The Urbana Free Library

To renew: call **217-367-4057**
or go to **urbanafreelibrary.org**
and select **My Account**

How Many Llamas Does a Car Weigh?

CREATIVE WAYS TO LOOK AT WEIGHT

by Clara Cella

PEBBLE
a capstone imprint

How many **llamas** does a car weigh? Two? Four? More, you say?

9
llamas!

Woohoo! Look who's come to play! How many **clowns** does a camel weigh?

8 clowns!

To measure the weight of this little **pup**, let's use hot dogs. Add them up!

16
hot dogs!

How many buttons does a **hummingbird** weigh? Quick, before it flies away!

3 buttons!

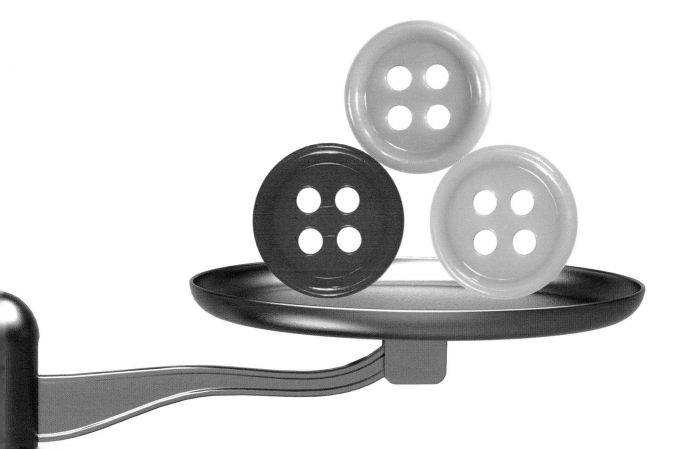

Now here's
a fact that's
pretty great:

A baseball and a bunny are the same weight!

Burgers are for lunch today! How many chipmunks does one weigh?

4
chipmunks!

How heavy is
a **moose**?
Do you know?

5
motorcycles, ready to go!

How many **birds**, beak to feet, weigh the same as this fruity treat?

10 birds!

LOOK FOR OTHER BOOKS IN THE SERIES:

How Many Ducks Could Fit in a Bus?

CREATIVE WAYS TO LOOK AT VOLUME
by Clara Cella

How Many Flamingos Tall Is a Giraffe?

CREATIVE WAYS TO LOOK AT HEIGHT
by Clara Cella

How Many Kittens Could Ride a Shark?

CREATIVE WAYS TO LOOK AT LENGTH
by Clara Cella

Pebble Sprout is published by Pebble, an imprint of Capstone.

1710 Roe Crest Drive, North Mankato, Minnesota 56003

www.capstonepub.com

Library of Congress Cataloging-in-Publication Data is available on the Library of Congress website.

ISBN 978-1-9771-1325-2 (library binding)

ISBN 978-1-9771-2012-0 (paperback)

ISBN 978-1-9771-1329-0 (eBook PDF)

Summary: Llamas, hot dogs, and six other silly, non-standard measuring units demonstrate the math concept of weight. Pre-readers learn the weight of a car, a hummingbird, a burger, and more through the use of surprising composite photos and a bit of text.

Image Credits

Shutterstock: Aaron Amat, 3 (right), Anan Kaewkhammul, 8, Artem Avetisyan, cover (bow), 1, BlureArt, 29 (red motorcycle), Chattapat, 17, cynoclub, 31 (gray and yellow bird), DC Studio, 7, 9, Dimitris Leonidas, 29 (white motorcycle), Don Fink, cover (llama), 1, Elnur, 9 (clown with yellow bows), Eric Isselee, 3 (left), 5 (brown and white llama), 11, 12, 25 (left, middle left, right), 31 (gray bird), Evgeniya Chertova, 29 (black motorcycle), Gena73, 23, 24, Ljupco Smokovski, 9 (clown in red), Maria 81, 27, 28, mariait, 5 (white and tan llama), photomaster, 5 (light brown llama), Praisaeng, 31 (yellow bird), Rawpixel, cover (top), back cover, 4, Stargazer, 15, 16, stock_shot, 25 (middle right), tobkatrina, 31 (bird with turned head), trekandshoot, 20, Tsekhmister, 19, 21, Valentina Proskurina, 31 (pineapple), Valentina Razumova, 13, vipmen35, 9 (balancing clown), yakiniku (scale), 4–5 (bottom) and throughout

Editorial Credits

Editor: Jill Kalz; Designer: Ted Williams; Media Researcher: Svetlana Zhurkin; Production Specialist: Katy LaVigne

Printed and bound in the USA.
PA99